WHAT MAKES A DEGAS
A DEGAS?

Richard Mühlberger

The Metropolitan Museum of Art

Viking

NEW YORK

VIKING
First published in 1993 by The Metropolitan Museum of Art, New York, and Viking, a division of Penguin Books USA Inc., 375 Hudson Street, New York, New York 10014, U.S.A. and Penguin Books Canada Ltd., 2801 John Street, Markham, Ontario, Canada L3R 1B4

Produced by the Department of Special Publications,
The Metropolitan Museum of Art
Series Editor: Mary Beth Brewer
Front Cover Design: Marleen Adlerblum
Design: Nai Y. Chang
Printing and Binding: A. Mondadori, Verona, Italy

Library of Congress Cataloging-in-Publication Data
Mühlberger, Richard. What makes a Degas a Degas? / Richard Mühlberger.
p. cm.
"The Metropolitan Museum of Art."
Summary: Explores such art topics as style, composition, color, and subject matter as they relate to twelve works by Degas.
ISBN 0-87099-674-6 (MMA) ISBN 0-670-85205-8 (Viking)
1. Degas, Edgar, 1834–1917—Criticism and interpretation—Juvenile literature. 2. Painting, French—Juvenile literature. 3. Impressionism (Art)—France—Juvenile literature. [1. Degas, Edgar, 1834–1917. 2. Painting, French. 3. Art appreciation.] I. Metropolitan Museum of Art (New York, N.Y.) II. Title.
ND553.D3M84 1993 759.4—dc20 93-7580 CIP AC
10 9 8 7 6 5 4 3 2 1

ILLUSTRATIONS

Unless otherwise noted, all works are by Edgar Degas and in oil on canvas.

Pages 1 and 2: *The Dance Class*, 32¾ x 30¼ in., 1874, The Metropolitan Museum of Art, Bequest of Mrs. Harry Payne Bingham, 1986, 1987.47.1.

Page 6: *Self-Portrait*, oil on paper, laid down on canvas, 16 x 13½ in., The Metropolitan Museum of Art, Bequest of Stephen C. Clark, 1960, 61.101.6.

Page 8: *Study of a Draped Figure*, graphite heightened with white gouache on beige paper, 11½ x 8⅞ in., The Metropolitan Museum of Art, Rogers Fund, 1975, 1975.5.

Page 8: Jean-Auguste-Dominique Ingres, *Study of Classical Drapery*, black chalk, estompe, partially squared off in black chalk, on beige paper, 19⅜ x 12⅝ in., The Metropolitan Museum of Art, Gustavus A. Pfeiffer Fund, 1963, 63.66.

Page 9: *At the Milliner's*, pastel on pale gray wove paper, adhered to silk bolting in 1951, 30 x 34 in., 1882, The Metropolitan Museum of Art, H. O. Havemeyer Collection, Bequest of Mrs. H. O. Havemeyer, 1929, 29.100.38.

Page 10: *The Bellelli Family*, 78¾ x 98⅜ in., 1858–67, Musée d'Orsay, Paris, © PHOTO R.M.N.

Page 13: *Giulia Bellelli*, essence on buff wove paper mounted on panel, 15⅛ x 10½ in., Dumbarton Oaks Research Library and Collections, Washington, D.C.

Page 14: *A Woman Seated Beside a Vase of Flowers (Madame Paul Valpinçon?)*, 29 x 36½ in., 1865, The Metropolitan Museum of Art, H. O. Havemeyer Collection, Bequest of Mrs. H. O. Havemeyer, 1929, 29.100.128.

Page 19: *Carriage at the Races*, 14⅜ x 22 in., 1931 Purchase Fund, Courtesy, Museum of Fine Arts, Boston.

Page 21: Utagawa Hiroshige, *Mochizuki Station*, from the series *The Sixty-nine Post Stations of the Kisokaido*, color woodblock print, 9¾ x 14⅞ in., ca. 1835, The Metropolitan Museum of Art, Purchase, Joseph Pulitzer Bequest, 1918, JP 585.

Page 22: *The Orchestra of the Opéra*, 22¼ x 18¼ in., Musée d'Orsay, Paris, © PHOTO R.M.N.

Page 25: *The Ballet from "Robert le Diable,"* 26 x 21⅜ in., 1872, The Metropolitan Museum of Art, H. O. Havemeyer Collection, Bequest of Mrs. H. O. Havemeyer, 1929, 29.100.552.

Page 26: *Race Horses at Longchamp*, 13⅜ x 16½ in., S. A. Denio Collection, Courtesy, Museum of Fine Arts, Boston.

Page 28: *Portraits in an Office (New Orleans)*, 28¾ x 36¼ in., 1873, Musée des Beaux-Arts, Pau; photograph, Marie-Louise Perony, Pau.

Page 33: *The Dance Class*, 32¾ x 30¼ in., 1874, The Metropolitan Museum of Art, Bequest of Mrs. Harry Payne Bingham, 1986, 1987.47.1.

Page 34: *Sketch of a Ballet Dancer*, brush and india ink on pink paper, 12⅜ x 17½ in., The Metropolitan Museum of Art, Robert Lehman Collection, 1975, 1975.1.611, recto.

Page 34: *Two Dancers*, dark brown wash and white gouache on bright pink commercially coated wove paper now faded to pale pink, 24⅛ x 15½ in., 1873, The Metropolitan Museum of Art, H. O. Havemeyer Collection, Bequest of Mrs. H. O. Havemeyer, 1929, 29.100.187.

Page 35: *Seated Dancer*, graphite and charcoal heightened with white on pink wove paper, squared for transfer, 16⅛ x 12⅞ in., The Metropolitan Museum of Art, H. O. Havemeyer Collection, Bequest of Mrs. H. O. Havemeyer, 1929, 29.100.942.

Page 35: *The Ballet Master, Jules Perrot*, oil on brown wove paper, 18 15/16 x 11 15/16 in., 1875, Philadelphia Museum of Art, The Henry P. McIlhenny Collection in Memory of Frances P. McIlhenny.

Page 36: *Miss La La at the Cirque Fernando*, 46 x 30½ in., 1879, reproduced by courtesy of the Trustees, The National Gallery, London.

Page 37: *Study for Miss La La at the Cirque Fernando*, black chalk and pastel, 18½ x 12½ in., 1879, The Barber Institute of Fine Arts, The University of Birmingham.

Page 38: *A Woman Ironing*, 21⅜ x 15½ in., 1873, The Metropolitan Museum of Art, H. O. Havemeyer Collection, Bequest of Mrs. H. O. Havemeyer, 1929, 29.100.46.

Page 39: *Woman Ironing*, 32 x 26 in., Collection of Mr. and Mrs. Paul Mellon, © 1993 National Gallery of Art, Washington.

Page 41: *The Singer in Green*, pastel on light blue laid paper, 23¾ x 18¼ in., The Metropolitan Museum of Art, Bequest of Stephen C. Clark, 1960, 61.101.7.

Page 43: *The Millinery Shop*, 39⅜ x 43⅝ in., 1879–84, Mr. and Mrs. Lewis Larned Coburn Memorial Collection, 1933.428; photograph © 1992, The Art Institute of Chicago. All Rights Reserved.

Page 44: *Dancers, Pink and Green*, 32⅜ x 29¾ in., The Metropolitan Museum of Art, H. O. Havemeyer Collection, Bequest of Mrs. H. O. Havemeyer, 1929, 29.100.42.

Page 47: *Self-Portrait* (?), photograph, The Metropolitan Museum of Art, Gift of Mrs. Henry T. Curtiss, 1964, 64.673.7.

Page 49: *The Rehearsal of the Ballet Onstage*, oil colors, freely mixed with turpentine, with traces of watercolor and pastel over pen-and-ink drawing on cream-colored wove paper, laid on bristol board, mounted on canvas, 21⅜ x 28¾ in., The Metropolitan Museum of Art, H. O. Havemeyer Collection, Gift of Horace Havemeyer, 1929, 29.160.26.

CONTENTS

SELF-PORTRAIT

Meet Edgar Degas

Hilaire-Germain-Edgar Degas was born on July 19, 1834, in Paris, France. He had an American-born mother from New Orleans, Louisiana, and a half-French father from Naples, Italy. Degas's father was a banker who considered it essential to expose his son to music and art. Known from the start as Edgar, the future painter attended an elite boarding school for boys named the Lycée Louis-le-Grand. Soon after he graduated, he announced that he wanted to be a painter, causing a major rift with his father.

Degas then went off on his own and lived a life of great privation in an attic room. He so impressed his father with his seriousness that they reconciled, and from then on Degas always had the full support of his parents. He attended art school in Paris, and then traveled through Italy, where he drew copies of the great paintings and sculptures of the past. This was the traditional way to complete a course of study in art.

Degas forged enduring friendships at school and was always loyal to family members. He made an informal family of his colleagues from the Lycée Louis-le-Grand and artist friends. To them, he was as famous for his cantankerous personality and his complaining as he was for his spectacular talent for drawing and painting.

The Old Master of the Impressionists

Degas is celebrated as one of the French Impressionists, a famous, informal group of artistic revolutionaries that included Claude Monet, Berthe Morisot, Camille Pissarro, and Pierre-Auguste Renoir. When he was young, Degas enjoyed spending hours on end with them talking about art. He helped organize their exhibitions, hung his paintings with theirs, and respected their concern for painting subjects from everyday life. But he did not accompany them on painting excursions. The Impressionists painted out of doors; Degas preferred working in his studio. They usually painted quickly; he was much slower. They enjoyed landscapes; he painted very few. They liked spontaneity; he planned more. They worked directly on their canvases with paint; he prepared detailed drawings on paper before he painted anything. They did not even share the same heroes in art.

Degas forever sought to learn the techniques of the Italian Renaissance artists Leonardo da Vinci, Raphael, and Michelangelo, and other

STUDY OF A DRAPED FIGURE

Degas admired Ingres above all other artists, and he practiced drawing as his idol did. Figures like these resemble Greek statues, which were considered to embody the highest ideals of beauty.

Jean-Auguste-Dominique Ingres
STUDY OF CLASSICAL DRAPERY

8

celebrated artists of the past. As a young man, he met Jean-Auguste-Dominique Ingres, a painter fifty-four years his senior, who worked in this tradition. Ingres drew with solid, graceful lines. Seeing Ingres's work increased Degas's belief that drawing must be the foundation of his own art. In this, he sided with older generations instead of with his young contemporaries who expressed themselves more with color than with line. After a few tries at painting classical themes, such as scenes set in ancient Greece, he curbed the impulse to imitate the subjects that his heroes had painted, realizing that they were out of date. Instead, Degas began specializing in scenes of modern life, allying himself more closely with his Impressionist friends.

Degas always bridged two worlds, the fresh, new world of Impressionism and the solid, traditional one of the Old Masters. Perhaps he would not have called himself an Impressionist, but he very likely would have enjoyed being known as the Old Master of the Impressionist group.

AT THE MILLINER'S
Modern life was a new subject for writers and artists. Never before had the public seen an ordinary place like a hat shop from an artist's point of view.

The Bellelli Family

Even as a young man, Edgar Degas excelled at certain things. None of his contemporaries, for example, could match him in portrait painting. When Degas complained that he was bored with painting people's faces, his father urged him on. He insisted to his son that "portraiture will be the finest jewel in your crown." During the first two decades of the artist's career, nearly half of his paintings were portraits, mainly of his family and himself. Degas set out to capture not only appearances, but personality traits as well, and he succeeded. His first great masterpiece was the disturbingly frank portrayal of his aunt Laura with her daughters and husband. The painting is called *The Bellelli Family*.

Degas's aunt, Laura Degas Bellelli, stands in a regal and protective way, staring sadly past her children and husband. Ten-year-old Giovanna, restrained by her mother's hand on her shoulder, crosses her hands nervously and stares straight ahead. Her seven-year-old sister, Giulia, screws her fists to her waist and looks toward her father. Arranged in a triangle, and dressed in black and white, they form a strong, united group. Baron Gennaro Bellelli is shown apart from them, next to the desk and in front of the fireplace. Degas had the gift of catching candid moments. He pictured the family not posing, but getting ready to pose for a portrait.

Degas said that he experimented with tones of black and white in the painting. His aunt's father had just died, so Laura Bellelli was dressed in mourning. The death also explains the black dresses her daughters wear. Degas placed a portrait of the deceased prominently on the wall next to his aunt. On the far left is a bassinet draped in white, for the baroness is pregnant. There is also a white candle on the mantel, waiting to be lit. Degas echoed its shape and color in Giulia's one exposed leg. Perhaps he thought the girls and the bassinet represented

light and new life, a happy thought amid the black cloud of unhappiness that had long hung over the family.

Degas's Italian relatives had been expelled from Naples, their native home, because of Baron Bellelli's revolutionary activities. After almost nine years of living in exile, the family returned to Italy and rented a furnished apartment in Florence. In 1858, Degas visited them there. The artist probably never saw his relatives together as he eventually pictured them. Instead, he drew and painted them individually and in groups, and later referred to his studies as he pieced together a composition for his eight-foot-wide canvas. Most of the labor was done in Paris.

Living far from home and in much poorer circumstances than they had been accustomed to, the family members seem uncomfortable in their new surroundings. Degas lived in the apartment with the Bellellis during his stay in Florence, so he was acutely aware of the tensions his relatives were experiencing. He chose to show them silent, withdrawn, and detached from one another.

OPPOSITE:

GIULIA BELLELLI

In preparation for his paintings, Degas made numerous sketches and drawings. They helped him decide how everything would look in the finished work. Here he concentrated on the posture of his cousin. He may or may not have instructed her to rest her hands at her sides, but it seems like a natural pose for an active girl trying to sit still for her talented relative. But when set into a family portrait, the turn of her head and position of her hands seem to be a reaction to her strict mother.

A Woman Seated Beside a Vase of Flowers

It is not unusual to see a painting of a woman with a vase of flowers nearby. But here Degas painted just the opposite. The bouquet appears front and center, and the woman leans into the picture from the side. It is assumed that she picked the flowers from the garden that can be seen out the window by her head. The gloves she wore to protect her hands are on the table next to a glass pitcher half filled with water. Having finished her first chore of the day, and slightly weary from it, the woman rests, content to think and plan in solitude.

The luxuriousness of the flowers sets the theme for Degas. He filled more than half the picture with their petals. Behind them, the wallpaper has a tamer and flatter floral design. Even the cloth that covers the table is decorated with flowers. In the background, dabs of pale color indicate flowers blooming in the garden, which can be seen through the curtained window. Throughout the painting, Degas created rich textures by making the flowers small and keeping them close together. The woman's gown is also textured, with waves of light and dark that make it look like crushed suede. Her hat and gown blend with the other colors in the picture. The only unornamented areas of the painting stand out: the woman's hand and face and the black scarf around her neck.

Through a Keyhole

At first glance, it may seem that the flowers are the primary subject of the painting, but after a second look, there is no doubt that the subject is the woman. Although she is partly hidden by the corner of the table, and the frame cuts off most of her left shoulder, arm, and hand, her presence is large. A spirited disposition and clever mind are suggested in the curve of her fingers, the placement of her hand, and the direction of her glance. Degas brought attention to the woman in an odd and daring way: by placing her almost out of the picture.

Degas wanted it to seem as though he and the viewer had just walked into the room where the woman is sitting. Later in his life, Degas said he liked his figures to look as though they had been seen through a keyhole. The feeling of immediacy became a hallmark of Degas's art. However, he was always quick to say, "Art was never less spontaneous than mine," an acknowledgment that his "candid" views were, in fact, very complex tricks. Nor was he ever known to paint a scene on the spot. *A Woman Seated Beside a Vase of Flowers* was composed the old-fashioned way, from drawings in his studio.

OVERLEAF:
Here Degas contrasts the lively and dynamic flowers with the subdued and introspective attitude of the woman. We do not know what she is thinking as she turns away from the bouquet.

Carriage at the Races

Paul Valpinçon was Degas's best friend in school and remained close to the artist all his life. Degas was a frequent visitor to his country house in Normandy, the northwest region of France, a long journey from Paris. Degas thought that the Normandy countryside was "exactly like England," and the beautiful horse farms there inspired him to paint equestrian subjects. During a visit in 1869, however, Degas found horses secondary to Paul Valpinçon's infant son, Henri. This becomes apparent by looking closely at the painting *Carriage at the Races*.

At first, Degas's composition seems lop-sided. In one corner are the largest and darkest objects, a pair of horses and a carriage. Against the lacquered body of the carriage, the creamy white tones of the passengers stand out. They are framed by the dark colors rather than over-whelmed by them.

Degas placed a cream-colored umbrella in the middle of the painting above some of the figures in the carriage. Near it, balanced on the back of the driver's seat, is a black bulldog. Paul Valpinçon himself is the driver. Both Paul and the dog are gazing at the baby, who lies in the shade of the umbrella. With pink, dimpled knees, Henri, not yet a year old, sprawls on the lap of his nurse while his mother looks on.

Ideas from the Exotic, Old, and New

Degas always enjoyed looking at art. One of the thrills of his school years was being allowed to inspect the great paintings in the collection of Paul Valpinçon's father. Throughout his life, the artist drew inspiration from the masterpieces in the Louvre in Paris, one of the greatest museums in the world. He also found ideas in Japanese

By cutting off, or cropping, the carriage on the left, Degas created the impression that the viewer is on the spot, glancing at the scene for the first time.

prints. They were considered cheap, disposable souvenirs in Japan, but were treasured by artists and others in the West as highly original, fascinating works of art. Photographs, then newly invented, also suggested to Degas ways of varying his paintings. He eventually became an enthusiastic photographer himself.

In *Carriage at the Races*, the way in which the horses and carriage are cut off recalls figures in photographs and Japanese prints. For Degas, showing only part of a subject made his paintings more intimate, immediate, and realistic. He wanted viewers to see the scene as if they were actually there.

Utagawa Hiroshige
MOCHIZUKI STATION
In Japanese prints, objects and figures were often arranged diagonally and cut off at the edge. Prints like this one inspired Degas to position important features in his paintings so that they were partially cut off by the frame.

The Orchestra of the Opéra

Few of Degas's many portraits were painted for hire. His subjects were primarily people he knew and liked, and this familiarity encouraged him to try new approaches. Désiré Dihau, the bassoon player in the orchestra of the Paris Opéra, asked Degas to paint him. He was Degas's friend and a frequent guest at the house of Degas's father at evenings devoted to music. Degas thought a great deal about how the portrait should look, discarding the idea of showing the bassoonist alone on a canvas. Instead, the artist decided to show him at work in the orchestra pit during a performance at the Opéra. The result is the illusion of a real moment in the musician's life.

The face of every man in the painting has been identified. Some were Opéra musicians, and others were friends of the artist, none of whom knew how to play an instrument. Degas made the nonmusicians look authentic by using characteristic poses he learned from watching the orchestra during many years of Opéra performances. Not only did Degas's painting make musicians out of men who were not, it also rearranged the orchestra's traditional seating. Ordinarily, Mr. Dihau's chair would be off to the left, behind the cellos and double basses. Here, he sits front and center. Degas once made a note to himself to someday paint the "swelling out and hollowing of the cheeks of the bassoonist." In this painting,

he convincingly caught Mr. Dihau's controlled breath as well as his practiced fingers.

Linking Dancers and Musicians

Degas portrayed a dozen or more men, all packed closely into the left side of the orchestra pit. One slanting line separates them from the audience, and another, from the stage. Both lines slope down to the right. The angle of the bassoon points up to the man at the far right who plays the double bass. The scroll of this instrument, in turn, links the men below to the women on the

stage. Formal attire peeks out from the crowd of men, while the bright white of Mr. Dihau's starched collar, tie, and shirtfront calls special attention to him. Though the top of Mr. Dihau's bassoon is hidden by the shoulder of the double bass player and the bottom of it is behind the divider, Degas showed more of his friend's instrument than anyone else's. This lively peek-a-boo view of the orchestra gives a much stronger sense of being there than it would have if every face and instrument had been arranged without overlapping.

Degas became famous for his pictures of ballet dancers, and this is the very first he painted. The dancers seem to be present here less for their beauty and grace than to provide a contrast to the musicians. The most obvious contrast is startling: The legs of the men do not show, but just the opposite is true of the women, whose heads and shoulders are cut off. The black wool and white linen of the men's clothing set off the dancers' pink and blue tulle. The light that illuminates the orchestra contrasts with the footlights on the stage. The brightest area of the dance is immediately above Mr. Dihau, and the deepest bend of a dancing leg perfectly imitates the angle at which he holds his bassoon.

THE BALLET FROM "ROBERT LE DIABLE"

Mr. Dihau is less conspicuous in this painting than in the glamorous portrait executed by Degas three years earlier. The bassoon player is in his regular seat, his profile silhouetted against a page of music.

Race Horses at Longchamp

Plaster sculptures of horses showing the animals' bones and muscles were often found in the large studios where students learned art. These models may have guided Degas in his first drawings of horses. Also, he rode frequently and thus knew, as he put it, "the difference between a purebred and a half-bred." French enthusiasm for purebred horses was born no earlier than Degas, and by the time he was an adult, it was as popular as it was in England, France's rival in horse breeding. Degas became a distinguished painter of racehorses, and he painted them many times.

On the west outskirts of Paris there is a large forest called the Bois de Boulogne. In 1856, a strip of land in the forest was given over to horse racing. It is called the Hippodrome de Longchamp. In this painting, Degas shows the racetrack at dusk. Following his usual method of constructing paintings in his studio, he based the images of the animals and their jockeys on drawings he had made a few years before. In fact, he often used the same drawing for a number of paintings. His skill hides his method. Here, the viewer is convinced that Degas was actually on the grass at Longchamp at the end of a racing day, watching the riders steer their steeds back to the stables.

Degas viewed the scene as though he were behind the horses on the right. By putting the stretch of trees between the jockeys' heads and the evening sky, he created an up-and-down play of colors. Degas repeated the pale yellow, blue, and pink from the sky in the shirts and caps of the jockeys. The soft light of dusk makes the colors glow. Degas gave each jockey the colors that best unify the various parts of the painting. He wanted the viewer's eye to go from the blue chevron-striped sleeves on the right to the blue caps and shirts on the left, and to find the patterns of white that link the riders with the stanchions defining the racecourse.

An Empathy for Horses

Degas was sensitive to the moods of horses. The patterns he created with the animals' legs against the turf emphasize the relaxed gait of the slow-moving creatures. They have done their work for the day and the pleasures of grain and grooming lie ahead. The horse on the far left, however, bolts. Degas originally painted his legs in another position before deciding to show him pulling to the left. The earlier paint marks still show, causing an animated effect that is like the double exposure of a photograph.

Portraits in an Office (New Orleans)

The New Orleans Family

Degas's mother had many relatives in New Orleans. They lured the artist's two brothers there to start a business, and Degas visited them in 1872. He traveled by paddle-wheel steamboat from England to New York, and then continued by train for four days. His trip was as intriguing to him as the city itself. "Everything attracts me here. I look at everything," he wrote to a friend in France. It is not known whether he painted anything other than portraits of the relatives he had come to see. He described them as "very affectionate but a bit free and easy with you, and who take you much less seriously because you are their nephew or their cousin."

Cotton was the business of his New Orleans relatives, and Degas discovered that they were engrossed by it. "One does nothing here . . . nothing but cotton, one lives for cotton and from cotton," Degas wrote. While he was visiting his uncle's offices one day, samples of cotton arrived from a plantation up the Mississippi River. This gave Degas the theme for the major project of his four-and-a-half-month stay in America. The painting that resulted, *Portraits in an Office*, turned out to be one of his most famous.

Degas viewed his uncle's office from one corner. In the upper left, a silvery rectangle marks one end of the long office. At the other end of the room is a tall panel of eighteen rectangular panes of glass, shining like mirrors. In between, the rhythmic patterns of glass panes, mullions, and frames march along the wall, turn the corner, and continue on, enclosing an inner office where two men work. The theme of rectangular patterns within a rectangular space continues in the shelves full of cotton samples at the far end of the office, in the fireplace, and in the frame of a painting of a ship that hangs above it. Every one of these straight-edged shapes is surrounded by the seafoam green of the walls and the warm shades of the floor and ceiling.

Recognition for the New Orleans Masterpiece

Degas told a close artist friend that the office interior scene was "a fairly vigorous picture." He could not have meant its mood or subject, because they are as relaxed as southern life. What must have been vigorous for Degas was fitting fourteen people into one canvas so all their faces would show! He used a trick learned from Japanese prints to make room for the full assembly of his male relatives and their chief employees and customers. He elevated the floor slightly from the far end of the office, which allowed everyone's head to show. Having some of the men in chairs and some standing also made it easier to arrange their faces and bodies into a realistic-looking scene.

Degas used the white of the clothing, paper, and cotton to lead the viewer's eye to critical areas in the office. His white paint is sometimes pure, and sometimes tinged with other colors. In each case, he used black close by to make the white seem whiter. The white cuffs and collar nearest the front of the scene belong to Degas's

uncle, the man in the top hat testing cotton. The white newspaper held by one of the artist's brothers is set against his dark clothing. Behind this figure, gathered around a long rectangle of cotton on a table, are the men who buy and sell this commodity. Degas put his second brother in shadows. With his legs crossed, he leans against the wall on the far left of the picture. A man less important to Degas, but essential to his family's cotton exchange, is the accountant on the far right. He wears the brightest white in the painting, and he is the largest figure in it. He is also conspicuous because of the detailed still life Degas made of his account books and wastebasket. Near them the artist decided to place his signature, the name of the city, New Orleans (using *Nlle*, the abbreviation in French for "new"), and the date, 1873.

Before the paint was dry, Degas returned to France. He hoped very much that his painting would be purchased by someone who would appreciate it, but for five years no one showed any interest. Finally, the work was shown in an exhibition in the small city of Pau, in the southwest corner of France near the Spanish border. The town's art museum then bought it. Degas wrote immediately to the museum's curator, "I must offer my warmest thanks for the honor you have done me. I must also admit that it is the first time that a museum has so honored me and that this official recognition comes as a surprise and is terribly flattering."

The Dance Class

Degas became the outstanding painter of dancers of his time, and few have ever matched him in painting the nuances of ballet preparation and performance. At about the time he was readying to paint *The Dance Class* and a few other major dance scenes, Degas met one of the greatest male dancers and choreographers, Jules Perrot. His strength and grace dominated the ballet stages of France and Russia in the 1830s and 1840s, and by the time Degas became a painter, Perrot was a renowned dance teacher.

Degas drew detailed studies of his new friend. They show the sixty-four-year-old man in a characteristic pose of a dance master, standing with legs astride, hands resting on a stout staff, and a practiced and critical expression on his face. Degas had made a great number of sketches of ballet dancers in every conceivable pose, and from these he created an imaginary class for the great teacher.

Degas could have posed Mr. Perrot at an actual class at the Opéra, but he did not. His way of making pictures was not to capture the whole thing at once on the spot. That was the work of the photographer, he would have said. He preferred to imagine his picture, then make it come alive through a careful use of his drawings. Here he had to overlap figures that in his drawings appeared in their entirety, as well as change the sizes of figures so they would look convincing in the long practice room. The mirror in the middle cleverly focuses attention on Mr. Perrot. As the teacher stares at the prima ballerina, his expression and stance suggest that he is mentally noting ways in which his student can improve her arabesque.

An Arabesque to a Better Life

The five dancers close to the front of the painting are considerably larger than the dancing figure halfway back, yet they do not take attention away from her. Along with the music stand and the cello on the floor, they form a large in-and-out pattern. In the background, hands on hips, a dark-haired dancer stands on a platform, gazing out toward the dancing demonstration. Degas transformed the cluster of human beings and attractive objects that would ordinarily stop the eye into a pattern that instead moves the eye on. This pattern supplements his use of the bright mirror to direct the eye to the dancer and the dance master. These compositional techniques are further augmented by a surefire device for bringing the viewer to the middle of the painting: Degas left half the floor empty. Anyone who wishes can walk right back to Mr. Perrot and his student, if not with the feet, then certainly with the eyes.

SKETCH OF A BALLET DANCER

Degas knew the rehearsal halls and backstage areas of the Opéra, where the ballet made its home, but these places were often crowded, noisy, and hectic. He preferred to draw the young dancers who became his subjects in his studio, where they could "hold a pose" until he committed every detail he wanted to paper.

TWO DANCERS

34

The diagonal pattern of white skirts and pink satin dance slippers along the edge of the empty path of wood flooring leads to bleachers and the back wall, where the mothers wait. With fussy hats and wraps around their shoulders, they coach their daughters. Because ballet dancers almost always came from poor families, the exposure they received on the Opéra stage was a way to open doors to a better life.

SEATED DANCER

RIGHT:
THE BALLET MASTER, JULES PERROT

Jules Perrot, once a great star of the ballet but retired at the time this oil sketch was done, did not mind posing while Degas captured the most characteristic details of his posture, costume, and appearance, as well as patterns of light and shadow across his clothing. When Degas was ready to paint Perrot, he could do so without worrying that his model would get tired, for the sketch took the place of the man. In his painting, Degas changed little from the study: He put a white handkerchief in the old man's pocket and made his staff solid to the floor. He also changed the gesture of Perrot's hand from one that questions to one that accepts.

Miss La La at the Cirque Fernando

Like many of his Parisian contemporaries, Degas was captivated by the daring acts of the circus. These were not the traveling shows with tents for theaters, but permanent establishments. The Cirque Fernando was the most famous, and Degas visited it often in January of 1879 to make drawings of the acrobat Miss La La.

Degas must have recognized the practice and effort that went into Miss La La's sensational act. Holding a rope by the strength of her jaws, the young performer was hoisted high above the audience to the rafters of the circus pavilion. She moved her arms and legs in a hypnotizing ballet as the hushed spectators craned their necks to follow her dangerous upward progress. Night after night, Degas drew her at the culmination of her act. Back in his studio, he produced this surprising painting.

Danger is suggested by the hot color of the circus ceiling, which spills onto the arms and legs of the acrobat like the reflections of flames, and clashes with her own pink costume. Miss La La's off-center position and Degas's viewpoint from below result in a dizzying imbalance. The angles of her arms, lower legs, and feet echo those of the roof beams. The disorienting composition makes viewing the painting as tense and exciting an experience as being next to the artist on the floor of the Cirque Fernando.

Degas's painting was carefully planned. After sketching Miss La La, he divided his drawing into squares. Next, he divided his canvas into the same number of squares, then he copied one square at a time from the sketch to the canvas.

Woman Ironing

Degas and his Opéra-going male friends all wore immaculate white, starched shirts, but they never saw them being laundered. That was done in

A WOMAN IRONING

places out of their sight, in the basements of their homes or in the back rooms of laundry shops. However, modern writers of Degas's time wanted to explore themes of everyday urban life, and took an interest in the poor women of Paris who laundered shirts and did other menial tasks. These novelists may have inspired Degas to explore this new and unusual subject. In 1869, he drew a model posing as a laundry girl ironing, and in 1876, he took up the subject again. This time, he did not hire a model to act out the role. Instead, he went to a laundry shop.

It is likely that Degas made drawings in the company of laundry women for some time, for when he showed them to one of the great writers of his day—a man famous for his descriptions of the working men and women of Paris—the writer was amazed at their truthfulness. Degas could even imitate the speech of the laundresses, and also knew the various strokes of the iron itself! He evidently had a gift for memorizing what he heard as well as what he saw.

Degas showed that ironing was hard work. The electric iron had not yet been invented; the crude instrument that the laundress grasps in her right hand is made of heavy cast iron and was heated by a coal-fired stove. A wood handle protected the laundress's hand from burns and made it easier to set a tepid iron back on the stove and

reach for a hot one, for a few reserves were always waiting. A laundress had to perform this motion many times before a shirt was finished.

Degas's Starched Shirt

Degas arched the back of the laundress, splashed light across her shoulders, and made her right

arm rigid to show that it takes work to make the iron glide. Reddened knuckles also show the harshness of her job. Her left hand deftly tugging wrinkles from the bright white shirt reveals her experience. A further testimony to her skill is the starched and folded shirt on her left.

With only one shirt done and many more drying on the lines across the windows, it must be the start of the day. Degas wanted to give the illusion of morning sun penetrating the half-wet shirts and illuminating the laundry room. To do this, he first painted the yellow-white curtains and the rose, ocher, lavender, and blue shirts. He then scraped off the paint so that just colored stains remained. He completed his painting by adding glazes, or layers of transparent colors, to show translucent cloth against light. His experiment worked. Sunshine floods into the room through layers of fabric. It illuminates the worktable, surrounds the laundress, and silhouettes her face.

In an ironic contrast, Degas made the hanging laundry look more wearable than the starched, folded shirt on the table. Rolled cuffs, a stand-up collar, a slit for a front opening, and sharp, rectangular folds make it look as if it were carved out of marble instead of sewn out of fabric. The starched shirt is totally rigid in a place where everything else is soft.

Stiffly starched shirts were the fashion for upper class men in Paris during Degas's time. This detail shows how Degas used a variety of colors to create a white shirt.

The Singer in Green

At night Degas found diversions from his art and, at the same time, sought new subjects for it. A host of noisy, flashy, and crowded entertainment spots attracted him. They were the cafés-concerts, or "caf'conç's," as they were familiarly called by the many people who enjoyed them.

Combining a drinking hall where refreshments were cheap, a restaurant with good food, and a stage for comic and sentimental entertainment, Paris's cafés-concerts had a loyal following. Degas frequented the fancier establishments, where famous singers were accompanied by full orchestras.

Drawing with Color

Before electricity was widely used in theaters, performers were illuminated from below by the flames of burning gas jets that lined the front edges of stages. Degas seemed to like the eerie effect of this flickering, unnatural light, so different from daylight coming from above. His youthful singer stands close to these unfriendly footlights, which throw shadows on her sloping shoulder and highlight her collarbone. Shadows also reach her face, circling her eyes. She is made to appear thinner and more fragile than she really may have been. The unkind illumination robs her flesh of color, but does not diminish the expressiveness of her black eyes. The bold gesture of her left hand contrasts strongly with the limp, uncertain attitude of her right hand.

Garish colors are made more strident by the flickering gaslights, and Degas seemed to delight in coloring the singer's skirt. Her golden-yellow bodice glows like brassy metal, and there is a

similar intensity to the color of the ribbons at her throat and in her hair. The palette of the gaudy costume served Degas for the background, too. The agitated marks of his pastels probably represent stage scenery or the outdoor garden of one of the cafés that Degas visited in summer.

By the time Degas made this drawing, he was working more often in pastels than in oil paints. Pastels gave Degas the opportunity to draw with pure color. There was no waiting for them to dry, as with paints. Though they look like crayons, pastels contain no wax, and therefore have no sheen. Degas liked their matte finish. Today the term "pastel colors" refers to soft and delicate hues, but Degas's pastels were strong and vibrant. They also gave him the freedom to scribble and smudge colors in the background.

In his letters, Degas mentioned particular singers with enthusiasm, commenting that one had "the most spiritually tender voice imaginable." He drew and painted a number of them.

The eager-to-please singer whom Degas drew with pastels seems young enough to be at the start of her career. Her face has not been identified as one of the known entertainers of the day, but she resembles a model Degas used for some dance subjects. The gesture of her left hand is also known; one of Degas's favorite singers used to tap her shoulder that way at the end of her songs in invitation of applause. It is possible that he combined drawings and mental pictures from various performances, while a model in his studio posed as the singer. Degas created an image of a girl leaving innocence behind and awakening to her power over an audience.

The Millinery Shop

Perhaps it was the artificial nature of women's hats that inspired Degas to turn to these fashionable accessories of Parisian modern life as subject matter. If the legend is true, Degas was not brave enough to enter a millinery, or hat shop, on his own, but his friend Mary Cassatt, the American painter, let him accompany her. Many paintings of millinery shops followed.

Most millinery shops in nineteenth-century Paris were exclusive places reserved for wealthy women. Hats were displayed on stands, arranged on a table covered in velvet. Except for the woman and her colorful merchandise, this shop seems empty. The long sewing glove that extends up her right forearm and the pin between her pursed lips show that she makes the

hats she sells and is beginning to work on a new creation. Degas arranged her head and the table display so that a beautiful, ornate hat with hanging yellow-green ribbons is positioned like a colorful floral crown over her head.

The dark walls and drapes push the eyes forward to the springlike display, keeping all the attention in the front. Hats punctuate the entire width of the painting. Degas obscured two hats in shadow. The other four hats are spotlighted and are brighter than their surroundings. The stands that support them blend with the shadows of the background and seem to disappear, making the hats appear to float. Out of an unremarkable scene of everyday life, Degas created a lively design.

Dancers, Pink and Green

Degas's famous ballet paintings witness his enthusiasm for dance and his intimacy with the private backstage areas of the Paris Opéra, the huge complex where the ballet made its home. He was equally familiar with the theater's more public boxes and stalls, where he watched many performances. During his lifetime, he produced about fifteen hundred drawings, prints, pastels, and oil paintings with ballet themes.

In *Dancers, Pink and Green*, each ballerina is caught in a characteristic pose as she waits to go on the stage. One stretches and flexes her foot. Another secures her hair, while a third is almost hidden. The fourth dancer, who looks at her shoulder strap as she adjusts it, holds a pose that was a favorite of the artist and one he used in many paintings. An upright beam separates her from the fifth ballerina, who also turns her head but in the opposite direction, full of anticipation. Above her in the distance are the box seats, which Degas simplified into a stack of six red and orange rectangles along the edge of the canvas. The vertical beam the ballerina is touching extends to the top and the bottom of the painting. The multicolored vertical shapes behind the dancers represent a large, painted landscape used as a backdrop for one of the dances. It will provide an immaterial, dreamworld quality to the performance, as it does to the painting.

Imitation Charcoal Pencil Lines

Subscribers to the Opéra were allowed backstage in the theater, and some took advantage of this access to pester dancers. On the far side of the tall wood column is the partial silhouette of a large man in a top hat. He seems to be trying to

Degas studied a subject long and hard before he painted it, but he liked the modern idea of capturing a fresh and vital impression. Here he brings the viewer backstage. The seemingly rapid and sketchy way of applying paint was another way to make the painting seem spontaneous.

keep out of the way, but his protruding profile overlaps a ballerina. None of the dancers pay attention to him. They also ignore one another, for this scene represents the tense moments just before the curtain rises.

Degas discovered that with oil paints he could achieve the same fresh feeling conveyed with pastels. Although this painting took the same amount of time to finish as many of his others and was designed and executed in his studio, Degas wanted to make it look as though it had been executed quickly, backstage. To do this, he imitated the marks of a charcoal pencil with his brush, making narrow black lines that edge the dancers' bodies and costumes. Next, he used his own innovation of simulating the matte finish of pastels by taking the sheen out of oil paint, then filling in the sketchy "charcoal" outlines of his figures with a limited range of colors. The colors he used for the dancers extend to the floor and the background. The technique gives the impression that he applied the colors hastily while standing in the wings watching the dancers get ready.

The results of Degas's experiments could have been executed much more quickly had he used pastels instead of oils. What Degas wanted, however, was to make paint look spontaneous. This was part of his lifelong quest: to make viewers feel that they were right there, beside him.

In spite of the frustrations of badly failing eyesight, Degas worked for a dozen years after he finished *Dancers, Pink and Green*. It is hard to imagine the tragedy of a great painter going blind, but at the end of a brilliant career, it happened to Degas. Until his death in 1917, he spent a decade unable to see what he had painted.

As a young man, Degas wrote, "In art you love and you produce only what you are used to." He always practiced those words, sharing his world with everyone who loved art.

When Degas was in his early twenties, and again, some twenty years later, he copied the signatures of famous artists into his sketchbook. In the earlier version, he included his name, repeated in different styles as though the shaping of the letters might determine his success. His signature appears but once in the later book. It is written proudly and with confidence, the *s* identical to the *s* in Ingres's name. Degas had found his way, without abandoning the lessons of his heroes. His career as an artist brought Old Master techniques and an Impressionist point of view into the twentieth century. If visions went through his mind after his sight had gone, one might have been of his famous signature alongside those of all the other immortals of art.

Late in his life, Degas made portraits of his family and friends using a camera instead of canvas and paint. He may have posed for himself to create this thoughtful and reflective portrait.

What Makes a Degas

The moments before or after an event interested Degas as much
as the event itself did. He liked to portray scenes from modern life.

1.

2.

3.

4.

1. Degas cut figures off at the edge
   of the canvas, creating a candid
   effect.

2. As if viewing it from above,
   Degas tipped the stage upward to
   keep figures from blocking one
   another.

3. Degas used patches of brilliant
   color to increase the feeling of
   movement.

4. Large, open spaces move the eye
   deep into the picture.